First published 1980 by
Octopus Books Limited
59 Grosvenor Street
London W1

Produced by Mandarin Publishers Limited
22a Westland Road, Quarry Bay, Hong Kong

Printed in Hong Kong

ISBN 0 7064 1391 1

Educational and Series advisor Felicia Law

Old Farm, New Farm

by
Felicia Law

illustrated by
Phillipe Dupasquier

octopus

OLD
FARM

Hens

'Things have got very bad round here,' clucked the hens. 'We just sit around feeling broody all day. I can't remember the last time one of us laid an egg.'

'The hole in the roof is so large that the fox walks in as if he owned the place.' 'The roost needs mending and the pens need new straw.'

'Throw down a little gravel outside for us to scratch around in. We do like to peck on a few gritty worms.'

'Scatter some corn in the yard and we might think about some speckled brown eggs for your breakfast.'

Farm Dog

'I haven't been too busy lately,' said
Bounce 'but it looks as if you're going to
need a best friend.'
'I'll help drive the cows down the lane to
the milking shed.'

'And it doesn't take a lot of brain to
round up a few silly sheep.'
'When I'm on guard, there'll be no foxes
sniffing round the farmyard.'

'I'll come for a drive whenever you're in need of company, and give you the benefit of my advice on market day.'

'All I ask is a quiet spot on the fire rug at the end of a hard day.'

Sheep

'Is it our turn now,' bleated the sheep, as they watched the sheepdog creeping round the back of the flock.
'We're coming, we're coming.'

'How we hate this bath in the sheep dip, although we know it's good for us. That strong disinfectant will get rid of all the insects that have made a home in our wool.'

'We need these woolly coats on cold winter nights, even though we have moved down from the hills to this sheltered field.'

'When snow covers the grass, we shall need hay and turnips to eat.'

'The lambs will be born in the spring. We may need the vet to help a sick mother or a weak lamb.'

'When the warm weather comes you can shear off our thick coats.'

Cows

'About time too,' grumbled the herd. 'It's long past milking time. Our udders are swollen with milk and most uncomfortable.'

'Now we line up in the stalls and wait for you to fix the teat cups on. The pump sucks the milk into the bucket in short squirts.'

'We deserve our feed in exchange for all that milk we have just given you, after all, you can make butter and cheese as well.'

'We know the way to the cowshed without this dog chasing our heels. After all, we come this way every morning and evening.'

'A few extra vitamins for the pregnant cow will help her produce a sturdy calf.'

'Even the bull seems more cheerful now we've got our slim figures back.'

Dairy

'There's plenty of scrubbing to do round here,' called the dairy, 'I've seen too much milk go sour on this farm.'

'Clean out the old butter churn and beat the cream soundly until it turns into rich, golden butter.'

'Skim the cream from the basin, and beat it until it thickens. Spoon it over your apple pie tonight.'

'Heat the milk and leave it to cool. See how it separates into curds and whey.'

'Soon the curds will stiffen into lumpy white cheese.'

'And there's nothing like a glass of cool milk to nourish you.'

Pond

'A little attention to the pond would be welcome,' quacked the ducks.

'It's clogged with weed and the bottom is thick with slime.'

'If you dredge the channels clear,
the stream will start to trickle again and
the water will become cleaner.'

'Cut back the reeds and bulrushes so that we can reach the water.'

'Then we can take the ducklings for a swimming lesson.'

Fencing

'A lot of my poles have rotted away,'
cried the fencing, 'and my wiring is all
over the ground.'

'Cut new wood to the right length, and
replace my rotten staves.'

'Pull up the weeds that clog up my posts and that stop me looking well kept.'

'Stretch wire tightly between my posts so that the animals can't walk through me.'

'Plant some flowers round my posts so that I look colourful in summer time.'

'Give me a fresh coat of paint so I am clean and bright all year round.'

Farm Equipment

'Hey, I need attention,' shouts the muck spreader. 'You will need me to spread manure over the fields and put richness into the soil.'

'My blades are all rusty,' whined the plough. 'How can I turn over the earth and carve deep furrows?'

'My prongs are bent,' scolded the harrow. 'They can't scratch the soil into a fine powder.'

'My hopper is clogged with rotting leaves,' grumbled the drill. 'The seeds won't run smoothly into the furrows unless you clean me out.'

'And if you are all out of action,' sighed long meadow, 'it will be another quiet year for me.'

Tractor

'I shall get round to you all,' promised Farmer Field, 'but first I must repair the tractor.'

'It needs a new pair of big wheels, the sort that are grooved with deep treads to help them grip in the mud.'

'I need it to lift and carry, to pull and push. None of you will move far without the tractor.'

'It needs oil round the machinery, grease round the hubs, and a tank full of diesel oil to power it.'

'I need a driver's seat up in the cab. I can see a long way from up here. In my tractor I can move down the field without touching the crops.'

'In my tractor I can pull the muck spreader, the plough, the harrow and the drill.'

Combine Harvester

'Well, I can wait until last,' said the combine harvester patiently. 'I can wait throughout the spring while the seeds are being sown.'

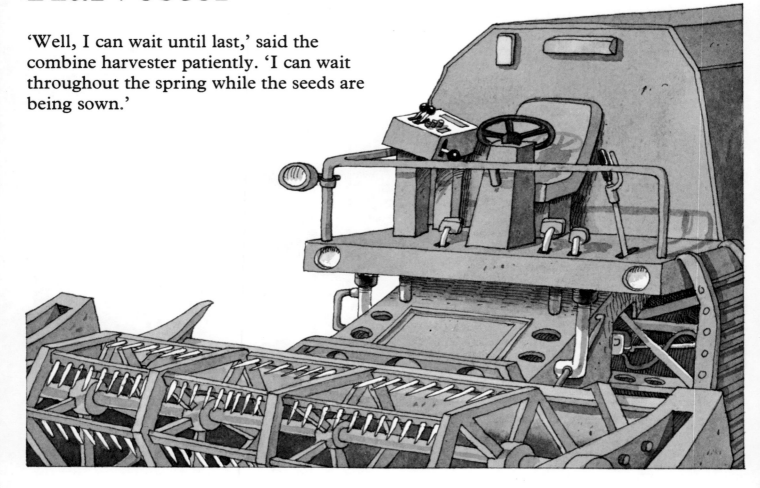

'I can wait all summer while the crops are growing and ripening.'

'But in the autumn you must sharpen my cutting blades ready for the harvest. I shall reap the corn, beating and churning it in my great stomach to separate the grain from the husk. I shall belch out the stalks of straw.'

Pigs

'To look at us now,' honked the pigs,
'you would think we had never seen a
three-course meal. Things will change for
the better now you have arrived.'

'We'd like a dry pig sty for a start. We'll
make a dust bath near the wood pile
where we can roll about and scratch the
odd tickle.'

'Two hearty meals a day of bran and leftovers will do us nicely, with a handful of apples and acorns for a special treat.'

'Just keep the mealtimes regular and we shan't trouble you again. We don't need much else in life.'

Barn

'Please mend the holes in my roof,' called the barn. 'The wind howls through all winter making the rafters creak.'

'There are owls roosting in the loft, cobwebs hanging in clusters from the beams and rats nibbling the corn.'

'Oil the hinges and the latch so that the great doors will close.'

'Brush out the loft. You can store fresh bales of hay up there for the winter feed.'

'Rake the floor and scatter fresh hay. During the cold months, the early lambs and kids can shelter here.'

'The barn cat will snuggle down for the night with her kittens.'

'Hang up the farm implements, the rake, pitchfork and feed buckets. There! Aren't things tidy?'

Orchard

'You'll get no fruit from us this year,' moaned the trees in the orchard, 'until you've pruned off these old branches.'

'In the spring we shall be covered with blossom.'
'Leaves and buds will sprout in the summer.'

'A light spray with disinfectant to kill the insects and disease in our wood would make us feel healthier.'

'Then our seeds will ripen into delicious fruit. We will fill your baskets with plums, pears and apples.'

Fruit Garden

'I can't take my job seriously,'
complained the scarecrow, 'when I've
nothing to do.'

'There's been no fruit on these bushes for so long,
the birds don't come here any longer.'
'You don't need to smarten me up, but
the bushes could do with a trim.'

'The blackberries have grown to bramble.'
'The raspberry canes need stout canes to climb.'

'Plant strawberries in rows, and cover them with netting once the fruit starts to ripen. That will make my job easier for a start.'

'This summer there will be fresh fruit and plenty left over for jam making.'

Beehives

'Nobody lives here any longer,' sighed the empty beehives.
'Could you set us upright on a strong platform?'

'Slot the ledges into each hive to make different sections.'

'Soon the queen bee will move into the bottom of the hive. Her eggs will hatch into bees.'

'The bees will fetch nectar from the summer flowers.'

'They will build combs of beeswax and store the nectar in them.'

'In autumn you must smoke the bees out of the hive and remove the honeycombs.'

'There will be golden honey for tea.'

Vegetable Garden

'Time to start weeding here,' announced the vegetable garden sternly. 'Loosen the soil with a fork and pull out these weeds.' 'Break the soil into fine crumbs with a hoe.'

'Plant the crops in neat rows. Sprinkle the seeds lightly through your fingers into the furrows.'

'Space the seedlings so that each has room to grow.'

'Water the plants when the weather turns dry. Spray them with insect killer to protect them from the hungry grubs.'

'Gather the beans and peas, the carrots and lettuce. If you don't take them, there's plenty who will.'

'Keep some vegetables for yourself and take the rest to sell at the market.'

Horses

'We need regular grooming and feeding', complained the horses, 'if we are to keep fit and healthy.'

'We would like to be put to some use. We just stand in this field, swishing flies with our tails.'

'Gone are the days when our coats were always glossy and we used to pull the plough or plough the headlands after the tractor had dug the furrows.'

'Sometimes we would take the farmer into town on market day.'

'If we are allowed to roam free once in a while, we'll be happy to help you should the machines break down or carry the children on our backs.'

Greenhouse

'Brrrr,' moaned the greenhouse, 'I shivered throughout the winter with these cracks and holes in my frame.'

'You could put that right in no time at all with a few panes of glass.'

'Soon the sun will warm me up and raise the temperature inside.'
'Set the plants out on the rack and spray them with water to keep them moist.'

'Soon the flowers will bloom and fat, red tomatoes will ripen on the canes.'

Farmhouse

'I'd like a coat of fresh paint inside and out,' requested the farmhouse.

'There are two cosy bedrooms under the roof, a large parlour at the front and a kitchen at the back.'

'A little spring cleaning will produce wonders.'

'Hang new curtains at the windows and set flowers on the table.'

'Home sweet home at the end of a hard day.'

AARON